AF481602

Table of Contents

Introduction

Breeding cannabis and continuing a lineage in seed is not the exclusive preserve of the experts. Home growers that have acquired high-level cultivation skills and mastered the essential techniques can easily transition from grower to breeder. Creating F1 seeds and hybrids is very doable. Most of the cannabis strains that have become legends were created by home growers. On occasion even by accident.

While it might not be possible to build your own seed bank from the grow tent in the spare bedroom. Small-scale breeding is a viable option. You don't need a masters degree in botany. Just good old-fashioned dope growing experience will suffice.

Time in the grow op will have already given you a keen eye for pheno hunting. Plus you have developed the hands on cannabis tradecraft skill set to succeed.

How to preserve precious marijuana genetics

Cloning

Taking cuttings from cannabis plants is a great way to preserve a strain. Sometimes prized varieties are available in clone-only form, and the grower has little option other than continuing to take cuttings in order to preserve the genetics.

Cloning is a transferable skill and even more essential to cannabis breeders than growers. You need to have a consistently high success rate with cloning as a prerequisite to breeding.

F1 selfing

Seeds can be produced with just a female marijuana clone. These seeds carry only the genetics of the mother. In order to accomplish this, the grower must reverse the sex of the female to induce self-pollination.

Most home breeders will purposefully stress the flowering female to produce a few seeds. Selfing is commonly applied to clone-only marijuana varieties to convert it to F1 seed form.

Small scale breeding options

Breeding from the same batch

Ok, so if you are happy with a batch of regular cannabis seeds. Perhaps you want to make use of the males? Well, you can cross cannabis from the same batch. Assuming you are familiar with the strain and cropping from the same pack of seeds you can potentially select a breeding pair to cross.

This is an old school ganja farmer's method mostly applied outdoors. Although, breeding from the same batch has potential indoors provided the original organic seeds are genuine. If so, not only will the resulting progeny be more or less stable but you will have saved cash on seeds for the next crop.

Before further breeding experiments, it's no harm to practice collecting pollen and making seeds first.

Breeding from a reliable batch is a good introduction to cannabis breeding.

Polyhybrids

A polyhybrid is simply a strain that results from crossbreeding two hybrid strains. When different landrace or inbred strains are crossed, this results in an F1 hybrid, a term used to label the first generation derived from the cross. F1 hybrids become F2, F3, and so on, as new generations are created via inbreeding.

However, if an F1 hybrid cultivar is bred with an F1 hybrid cultivar from a different genetic line, a polyhybrid is formed. F1 hybrids already possess varying genetic traits from both parent strains, meaning polyhybrids are even more diverse and unpredictable in the traits they possess. Creating polyhybrids is a great breeding method as it allows you to combine unique traits from a wide spectrum of cultivars. Although, as you can imagine, these strains are quite unstable and heterozygous. It takes some solid work to stabilise these varieties and ensure that their offspring are more uniform.

Breeding polyhybrids at home
Breeding cannabis requires quite a lot of space. You need a nursery and propagation area and different rooms for male and female specimens to avoid unwanted cross-pollination. Even more space is needed if you intend to start breeding polyhybrids over multiple generations starting with four inbred cultivars. If you intend to begin this process, you'll need to learn how to pollinate your flowers in the correct way.

Seeing as you're considering breeding, you are probably already well aware of this fact, but it's always worth reiterating: Keep your males away from your females! This is especially important when looking to breed a polyhybrid because of the increased chances of breeding the wrong varieties together.

First off, you'll need to collect pollen from male plants when the time is right. Pollen is ultimately plant sperm, and is needed to fertilise female flowers to make them produce seeds. When the male pollen sacs have opened, place a sealable bag over the plant and give it a shake.

Female plants are ready for breeding during the early flowering phase when small, white pistils start forming. These "pre-bud" structures are basically little hairs that protrude from the calyx to catch pollen. Next, isolate the chosen female plant to further prevent any unwanted fertilisation. Consider setting up a specific fertilisation area to avoid any mishaps.

To pollinate female plants, place the pollen bag over branches that show bud formation. Seal the bag over individual branches and shake again. Leave it there for around 1 hour and repeat the process with each branch that bears buds.

It's vital to document everything you do when breeding cannabis, especially during the more complex process of creating polyhybrid strains. It's easy to mix up genetics and lose track of which male you bred with which female, and what strain each of them is. It's best to label every plant individually so they can be easily identified. It's also a good idea to create a spreadsheet or draw out a flowchart on a whiteboard to keep track of every cross you've made with each individual plant. Add dates beside every documented task to help you estimate waiting periods accurately.

Genuine f1 hybrids

Genuine F1 Hybrids are the jewels in the crown of the Royal Queen Seeds catalogue. The cold truth is creating fantastically potent, productive and vigorous growing F1 hybrids is a long term process. Professional breeders invest years of their lives into breeding projects and select cultivars from hundreds if not thousands of cannabis plants.

Genuine F1 hybrids can only be derived from crossing pedigree stabilised or landrace strains. They express genuine hybrid vigour. Unless you're planning a strain hunting expedition, tracking down heirloom landrace seeds is hard graft. It's probably more convenient to stick with the RQS catalogue for awesome hybrids.

Similarly, filial breeding can be complicated. Honestly, it's far too demanding for the first time home breeder. By crossing a pair of F1s (first generation) the resulting progeny is the F2 (second generation). Unfortunately, these seeds will be far less stable and far more difficult to work with than the previous F1 generation.

Careful selective breeding in large numbers is required to succeed with this approach. Often it takes multiple generations of breeding perhaps until F5 (fifth generation) or even F6 (sixth generation) before the line can be stabilised.

Backcrossing
Have you ever purchased the same cannabis strain multiple times and noticed that it looked completely different each time? Maybe it even tasted slightly more sweet or sour than before. Or maybe you've grown the same strain repeatedly and realised how different one plant looked from the next? These differences within the

same strain are referred to as genetic variability. Even though plants share the same lineage, their unique genetic expression, or phenotype, is a result of how their genetics respond to the environment.

Differences in phenotypes can manifest as variability in size, resin production, colour, and so on. Strains can also vary in their chemotype. This refers to the chemical constituents that they manufacture. One plant might have higher levels of a specific terpene, whereas another may have slightly higher levels of CBD. If you germinated a bag of seeds that all shared the same lineage and noticed a large difference between the phenotype of each plant, this would mean that the strain is unstable, and that the seeds are heterozygous. Although this isn't necessarily an issue for hobby growers, it can become problematic for commercial growers looking for strict consistency among their crop.

This consistency is possible, and can be achieved by stabilising the genetics of a strain. This will then produce seeds that are more homozygous, featuring significantly less variability between phenotypes. But how can breeders go about stabilising a strain?

One way to achieve this is called backcrossing, also known as "BX" within the cannabis breeding lexicon. When breeders are aiming to create a new strain, they select two parent strains with desirable traits. Upon crossing them, the first generation is created. Backcrossing essentially refers to taking a member of this generation back up the family tree to breed it with one of its parent strains. This type of inbreeding helps solidify the presence of one of the parent's genes as they are bred together repeatedly.

For example, if the female parent strain was particularly high in CBD and myrcene, thus producing a calming effect, by breeding her with one of her male offspring that also shares some of these traits, the plants of the next generation would be even stronger in those traits. This is because they will contain more of her genetic material than the original generation that was also influenced by the male parent.

Although backcrossing is a tried and tested way to stabilise cannabis genetics, excessive backcrossing can cause some issues. By inbreeding plants to such a degree, any recessive genes that produce undesirable traits will also be strengthened and passed down to all plants of subsequent generations.

As you can see, there are quite a few ways to preserve your favourite strains, and turn them into new strains of their own. This guide is meant to give you a good general overview to get you started, before delving into the more complicated aspects of it.

Making feminized seeds
Growing cannabis is all about resinous flowers, trichomes, and rich cannabinoid profiles. These splendid characteristics can only be found on the female flowers. Having gardens full of robust, un-pollinated sinsemilla females means jars full of mind and body-friendly, crusty nuggets.

The only bummer, unless you grow from clones, is that cannabis is wired to produce about 50% male seeds and 50% females. It is just the nature of the beast.

Wouldn't it be sweet if it was possible to grow all females from seed, every plant, every time?

Well, that is where the feminizing technique comes into play: two methods of manipulating the cannabis plant to produce only females from seed, every-time. To be truthful, it isn't every single time. But 99% of the time is a pretty good number, and could be considered entirely male risk-free.

The general practice behind feminization is that female plants are forced to produce pollen, which is in turn used to pollinate other female plants. The outcome? Resulting seeds will be feminized, with no risk of further pollination.

Why feminize?
Feminized seeds are super efficient for indoor and outdoor gardeners. Area, time, and resources aren't being

given to plants that will be thrown away two weeks after the 12-12 flip. Similarly, outdoors where a large plant can consume a lot of time and resources in upkeep prior to the autumn show of flowers, feminized plants are also a good way to reduce guerrilla crop pollinating. There's nothing worse than bush-bashing out to a well-hidden crop only to find a rogue male or two have impregnated every female plant.

Inhibit that ethylene

"Applications that reduce the ethylene level in tissues or antagonise the action of ethylene causes the formation of male flowers instead of female ones" — Paraphrase, Byers et al., 1972.

There are a number of solutions that can be sprayed on female plants to create male pollen sacs: benzothiadiazole, gibberellic acid, silver thiosulphate, silver nitrate, and colloidal silver.

Colloidal silver is by far the easiest to source or make. It is non-toxic, non-caustic, and can be bought from a pharmacy or easily online. The other solutions can be dangerous, difficult to get a hold of, and expensive—except gibberellic acid, which can be found in nurseries, but is not as effective as colloidal silver. But if you want to watch some freaky plant growth just for the fun of it, give gibberellic acid a try. It is a growth stimulant and makes plants stretch and stretch.

Make feminized seeds

Technique 1: colloidal silver
Colloidal silver is a distilled water-based solution in which microscopic particles of silver are suspended. The nature of colloids means the particles will never settle out and can't be removed by normal filtering. Colloidal silver is available commercially, or you can make your own if you want to totally geek out (see how-to section at the end). It has numerous uses as an alternative medicine. For example, it is used to soothe burns, as an antiseptic and digestion stimulant in people, and as a fungal control in horticulture.

Be sure the strength is at least 15ppm, preferably 30ppm. Less than 15ppm produces male sacs with little viable pollen.

To begin with, select a plant that has the characteristics you want to preserved. Feminizing clones is the usual practice as the growth, flowering, and resin characteristics from the mother are already known. There is no need for any vegetation time once a clone is well-rooted. Simply pot the clone into a small pot, give it a day or two to recover, and begin a 12-12 light cycle right away. A pollen-producing plant only needs to be small as cannabis produces copious amounts of pollen.

Hint: Make two clones once a plant has been selected, one to be feminized and one to be left for pollination. This way, a separate breeding space is created and accidental seeding of other plants, or an accidental sneeze pollinating a whole grow cupboard, is avoided.

Plants can be induced to grow male sex organs as late as four weeks into flowering. Though spraying one week prior to the light changeover is recommended for clones.

If a plant grown from seed is being used, wait until the plant has sexed before spraying so you can be sure it is female.

Spray the plants to be feminized with colloidal silver every day, and three times a day if you can manage. Soak them well. Do this for two weeks, then leave the plants to grow as normal. Some growers report getting results after spraying for only 5–10 days.

When sexing begins, male pollen sacs will develop instead of female calyxes and pistils. Male plants mature much faster than females, and viable pollen can be expected within 3–4 weeks once the plant has been sexed. Some growers will spray until the plant shows sexual growth, just to be sure the method has worked. Make sure these plants are well-isolated from any flowering females. A burst pod can release millions of pollen spores, and it only takes one spore per hair to create a seed.

Don't smoke it

Once the plants have been sprayed with colloidal silver and the pollen is collected, they are write-offs—86 them and don't smoke them. Giving them a thorough rinse will not work. The colloidal silver is a systemic treatment absorbed into the plant through the foliage and not a topical application. Be safe and bin them.

Technique 2: rodelization

Sinsemilla is an unnatural state for cannabis. Without human intervention, it would be rare to find an unpollinated female in the wild—unless it was sterile. When sinsemilla plants are left to go beyond their desirable maturation stage by a number of weeks, the plant, through whatever amazing processes evolution has bestowed, knows it has not been pollinated. As a last ditch effort at propagation, it will produce male pollen sacs in an effort to self-pollinate.

This is not the result of genetic or stress-induced hermaphroditism. They are genuine XX chromosome male bananas. With all the genetic information from the female and no Y chromosome, using rodelized pollen creates female-only seeds, although as with colloidal silver, an occasional male may appear.

Harvesting pollen and pollination

There are a number of harvesting methods employed to catch pollen.

- Cover the top of the pot with plastic or card to catch pollen as it falls, or modify a plastic drink cup to shroud the plant and catch falling pollen.
- Fix a clear plastic bag, perforated at the top for air exchange, around the whole plant.
- An experienced eye will remove each flower pod prior to it bursting completely open to be sure of catching every spore.

Pollinating a female is the easy bit. Depending on how many seeds you want to make, there are a couple of methods that can be used.

Using a watercolour or other fine, soft brush or even a cotton bud, dip into your pollen collection and gently apply to the chosen flower. Although thousands of viable spores will be on the end of the brush, enough to pollinate a whole plant, the trichomes on the surface of the pistils will greedily glue everything you offer them. So dip into your pollen stash a few times as you dust.

For lots of seeds, put pollen in a bag and put over a whole branch or a whole plant, shake well, and leave for twenty four hours.

It is possible to pollinate different branches with different pollens and have a breeder plant that has 1, 2, or 15 different crosses on it.

It is also possible to self-pollinate the plant from which the male parts were created. This won't produce as many seeds as pollinating a separate plant because less female flowers are produced and many are nonviable because of the feminization process.

Growing feminized plants
Treat feminized seeds as you would any other seed from germination to veg, and veg through flower. Observation is where it's at now, you want the best plants for your

garden. Ideally, setting up a separate vegetation/flower space where a number of plants can be grown lets your standard grow space continue with uninterrupted production.

Plants bred using feminization are homozygous. This can have two effects that can't be assessed until the seeds are grown. Homozygosity will increase the dominant or recessive traits of the parent in the progeny, so features you don't want and do want can be amplified. Genetics is a weird, weird thing.

Just as with standard male to female crossings (which is a heterozygous process), a number of plants will need to be grown and the best selected for mother plants and future breeding. With enough room, hundreds if not thousands of new plants can be grown in order to select the best of the best phenotypes.

Fembots rule
With a bit of aforethought, it is possible to set up an efficient feminization breeding programme—and have

female seeds from your favourite phenos on hand all the time. You never know, you might discover the next big thing!

Making your own colloidal silver

The easiest and relatively inexpensive way—considering how much money is potentially saved by not growing resource and time-consuming males—is to buy a colloidal silver generator, which is the no-fuss plug and play option. Or, make your own, which is quite straightforward and doesn't require any special skill.

Colloidal silver is formed by passing a current from a pure silver electrode through distilled water. This simple electrolysis is all there is to it. Although distilled water does not conduct electricity very well due to its lack of mineral content, enough is passed through to create micro silver particles and silver ionisation. Sounds technical, but it really isn't.

What you will need

- A power adapter—9–12 volts is ideal, or a 9-volt battery. Higher voltages can be used, but you really need to know what you are doing so you don't get electrocuted.

- Electrical wire. One length for the positive and one length for the negative.

- Distilled water. This is easy to find at your local supermarket. Do not use tap water as it has too many impurities that can harm the process.

- Pure silver, at least 99% pure. Silver coins are ideal and relatively inexpensive. They are available on eBay, coin dealers, and mints. Silver wire gets results, with some reports that silver solder works also, although it is unknown what the other metals in these alloys might do. Going with a source of pure silver is safest.

- Small alligator or crocodile clips to hold the silver.

- A ppm meter.

- Make sure the adapter is set at 9–12 volts.

- Strip each end of the wires using scissors or wire strippers.

- Securely connect the alligator clips to one end of each wire to ensure a good flow of current. Soldering is best.

- Fix the wires to the positive (red) and negative (black) terminals on the unplugged adapter or onto the battery.

- Put a piece of silver in the jaws of each clip. Don't touch them together. Fill a glass jar or glass beaker ¾ full with the distilled water. 500ml will easily do two plants.

- Suspend each silver/alligator clip combo in the water on opposite sides of the glass.

- Plug in and turn on the adapter. If you are using a battery, the process began the moment the electrodes were submersed in the water.

- After 20 minutes, remove the electrodes and test with the ppm meter. 15ppm (0.5) and over is the goal. The solution should become a pale gold colour.

- When finished, clean the black silver oxide off the silver electrodes and put the kit into storage until next time.
- Store the colloidal silver in an amber-tinted bottle in a cool place. It is light and temperature-sensitive. However, don't put it in the fridge.

Basic Cannabis Knowledge: Genotype and Phenotype

Many growers tend to misuse the words genotype and phenotype when talking about cannabis. Let's clear the smoke around this issue and resolve all the unnecessary confusion.

There's a point in the life of every grower when suddenly questions arise. Most of the time, this moment of confusion comes right after completing the first couple of grows, and at the latest, when the same strain is repeatedly grown using the identical set-up.

Why in the world does every single cannabis plant grown from seed look slightly different?

When these or similar questions remain unanswered, a logical reaction for a rookie grower would be to switch to another breeder. The more experienced cultivators know that this phenomenon, meaning variations among different plants of the same strain, is natural and won't get any better by changing the seed supplier. We have to keep in mind that seeds are products of living organisms and the outcome of a natural breeding process, hence unique as any person, animal or plant on earth. Although it's tempting to characterize all the things around us, we're quick to reach limitations when dealing with nature.

Genotype, environment, phenotype
Every living organism is the result of evolution that works by the same basic principle. The genotype or genetic code carries all the genetic information regarding growth, appearance, and all the characteristics we can

later observe. It's crucial to understand that a genotype or genetic code is not something that is set in stone but rather defines a certain range of possibilities. It mainly depends on the environment the organism lives in what specific bits and pieces of the genotype will be activated. The interaction between genotype and environment results in a phenotype, meaning the physical expression of certain genes the environment triggered.

genotype (G) + environment (E) + genotype and environment interactions (GE) = phenotype (P)

Quick example: purple strains

Let's examine a cannabis related example to get a better idea. You purchase seeds from a reputable breeder and intend to grow a purple strain. Instead of growing all plants in your indoor grow tent, you'll decide on moving half of your plants outdoors. Besides the fact that no plant seems to be identical to one another, you'll notice that the plants in your outdoor garden are much richer in purple colours compared to the ones in your indoor grow tent. Although the genotype carries the information to produce purple hues, it's the environment, and in this particular case, the temperatures of the environment, that allow two different physical expressions (phenotypes) from seemingly the same genetic code (genotype).

The common misassumption

We got the idea that the environment is the determining factor influencing a genotype to express different phenotypes, but this doesn't answer the initial question why every cannabis plant grown from seed appears to be slightly different, even when it's grown in a constant environment of an indoor grow room.

How can a strain possibly express different phenotypes when the environment doesn't change?

Well, it's maybe an inconvenient truth, but every single cannabis seed has its unique genotype. Many growers assume that seeds from the same cannabis strain share an identical genetic code and understandingly expect homogeneous growth. Unfortunately, this is a common misassumption. There are lots of people using the term phenotype to describe the variations of plants they get from the same strain grown from seed. In fact, and what they usually don't know, they're talking about different genotypes. It's not only the environment that determines phenotypic expression, but logically also the genotype itself.

When you purchase seeds of a certain strain, you'll receive "family members" of this strain that share a large percentage of genetics with thousands of (inbred) siblings, yet they're not identical twins. The genotype is usually very close to identical, but there are still differences, comparable to fraternal twins if you will. That's the main reason why every cannabis plant grown from seed expresses slight variations regarding characteristics like plant height, yield, flavour, etc. – the genotype of seeds is usually not identical.

End the phenotype dilemma: seeds vs clones

If you want to take homogeneity to the next level, you have two different options. The first option is to germinate more seeds as you intend to grow, and simply select the ones that express the desired traits at an early stage. But if you're aiming for maximum efficiency and consistency, your best option is to select a mother plant to take clones from. These clones copy the genotype of the mother plant 1:1 and you'll continuously end up with the same phenotype assuming a constant environment. Let's say you grow one of these identical clones using a hydro set-up, and one in organic soil. This varying environment might result in different phenotypes of the same genotype.

Cannabis Plants: Male, female and hermaphrodite

Determining the gender of your cannabis plants is the first step to a successful grow. Female plants are the only ones that produce bud cannabis. While it is fairly easy to spot the gender difference, cannabis does come with a curveball. Plants can also be hermaphrodites. And female plants can switch to this state during growing stress.

Cannabis plants are not gender neutral. There are female plants, from which the actual bud flower comes. Male plants produce the pollen. However, the cannabis plant is a bit odd in this respect. Female plants can turn hermaphrodite in certain circumstances - meaning they are both male and female. This happens in a situation where the plant is highly stressed, and fears for its ongoing survival. It becomes both genders as a last resort to self-pollinate and continue to spread seeds.

Cannabis is from both mars and venus

Regular cannabis seeds are usually about 50% male and 50% female. The female plants produce bud cannabis. Male plants produce seed pods. They can also produce tiny amounts of THC via trichomes on the leaves. However, if you are not growing your cannabis as a science experiment don't mess with male plants. It is a waste of time.

Obviously, particularly to the non-expert, all seeds look alike. That is why it is so important when growing cannabis, to buy seeds from a dealer or seed bank. While the plant is in the early stages of growing, it is also impossible to determine gender.

There is only one more problem. Cannabis plants can be both male and female in the right circumstances.

Cannabis and the sexes

Cannabis is actually much like other plants - with most having this ability. In essence, female plants have the ability to develop male characteristics. This usually occurs thanks to environmental stress. Plants will develop male characteristics at a certain point in the grow cycle in an effort to ensure seeds are produced before the stressor can kill the plant.

Such stress includes changes to hours of darkness during flowering, dramatic changes in temperature, drought and physical damage.

There are other environmental factors which can stress a plant into a sex conversion. This includes as a reaction to insects or disease. It can also occur with the use or overuse of certain kinds of pesticides and fungicides.

However, this tendency is also considered to be a sign of inferior plants. A good mother plant will not show signs of hermaphroditism even when subjected to this kind of stress. All cannabis can turn, but high-quality genetics will resist the urge the most.

As in the human world, hermaphrodite plants are considered a bit strange. In the cannabis one, they are dreaded. Breeders suggest removing such plants from a grow. The reason? They could create accidental pollination of the buds. If a pollen sac from one of these plants is allowed to come in contact with the buds of other plants, those buds will stop developing. They will instead, produce more flowers and seeds.

When do cannabis plants show gender?

The first sign of gender appears at the V shape on the plant where stalk meets stem. The plant will develop little green shoots or pre-flowers here. The plant may show pre-flowers when in the vegetative or growing stage. This is also more the case when the plant is a clone.

However, there are other ways to find out if any of your plants are hermaphrodites. The first is to check the kind of flowers they produce. The second comes at the end of the growing process. However, it is important to check before you grow the next time. If you find seeds in your harvested bud and you know you have no males, you have a hermaphrodite plant.

What to look for
The first answer is an established breeder. The best way to start with an all-female crop is to buy the feminized seeds from an established source.

However, since this is a problem that will not disappear during the growing process, here are some guidelines for checking your grow.

Female plants take a bit longer than males to show signs of gender after flowering. The plants begin to develop a few wispy white hairs where the buds will soon grow. These flowers begin to form between the stalk and stem. Female pistils are always white (never green).

Male plants literally have grape-sized "balls" of pollen. The balls will show up about a week or two after the plant has entered the flowering stage. They also produce a growth that is a distinct yellow colour and look a bit like bananas.

If the male is allowed to continue growing, the pollen sacs will burst open. The pollen they spill can contaminate your other plants.

Hermaphrodite plants have both male and female flowers. That is also why it is so important to remove them.

Isn't this like rocket science?
While it sounds complicated, it really isn't. Growers who start with the right seeds and maintain a healthy grow environment do not have many problems. For this reason, however, it is important to watch your cannabis plants.

It is fairly easy to spot the difference in buds as the plants mature. That is also why it is generally a good idea to grow more than one plant – even the first time. Observation, practice and patience are the keys to a good and healthy grow. Feminized seeds produce femal plants 99% of time, and should one turn hemaphrodite, simply take care to remove it.

How to put your cannabis stems to good use
It's common to hear people associate cannabis stems with low-quality bud, and you might think they're nothing but a headache. Try saving them next time you find them, though. Whether you want some THC-kissed tea, cannabutter, hash, or even some twine or yarn, the

possibilities are nearly endless if you save them and know what to do.

If you're not the type to grind up your stems with your bud, you've either got a garbage bag full of them or an impressive collection. If you're in the former group, we've got some information that might make you reconsider. If you're in the latter, though, today just might be your lucky day.

What to do with your marijuana stems?
You see, those stems are a lot more than scraps to throw out when grinding your cannabis flower. In fact, if you store up enough, you can get plenty lifted off those alone. And, if you don't want to get high, you can even give them a second life as arts and crafts items, or even mulch! How? We'll cover the details as we go along.

Smoking
The simplest solution, although it's the least recommended, is to grind your stems up and smoke

them. This is always a harsh experience, and the smoke contains many unwanted compounds from the cellulose in the stems. The cellulose also makes stems burn extremely hot—more than enough to burn your throat and lungs. Again, it is not recommended, so please be careful. Very few people do this, but for some reason, some decide to light them up.

Charas

Hash doesn't get much more hands-on than this. To obtain charas, start by rubbing your stems between your hands. After that, rub your hands together over a container to get a whisker of hash. It won't be much in that moment. However, work through 100 grams of stems with average THC content, and you may be impressed at what you've managed to gather. The end result is a multi-flavoured pile of hash that's as old-school as it gets.

Kief

If you want to get this process started, just take your stems, break them down, and throw them into a resealable plastic bag. Place this bag in your freezer, and let it sit until you've got more to add. When you add to the collection, give the bag a healthy shake. Each time you shake, the now-frozen resin crystals will begin to detach from the stem fragments. Slowly but surely, you'll build up an impressive pile at the bottom of the bag. Once you sift out the stems, you'll have a whole bunch of kief ready to smoke!

Bubble hash

Similarly, if you want some quality bubble hash, the first step is freezing the stems. Rather than shaking, though, you'll be throwing these in a blender. Use the blender method recipe from our full guide to making hash—just replace "flowers" with "stems". If you follow all the right instructions, repeating the process about 4–5 times, quality bubble hash will be in your future.

Don't forget decarboxylation

Before anything, if you want to make use of the THC content of your stems, decarboxylation is key. It might seem like a confusing process based off the name, but it really just means you're heating them up to a certain point. This process creates the easily absorbable and immediately psychoactive THC from its precursor chemical, THCA. This, in turn, makes the stems perfect for tinctures, hash, extracts, and edibles.

To decarboxylate, evenly spread your stems on an oven tray and place in the oven at 110°C (or 100°C for a fan-assisted oven) for 60 minutes. Once decarboxylated, your stems are ready to go!

Tea and chai

To get started, you'll need a healthy handful of stems that have not been rubbed for hash. Start off by putting 450ml of water and a tablespoon of coconut oil into a small saucepan. Chop and add your stems and slowly bring to a gentle, but not rolling, boil, stirring continuously. Let them boil like this for 7 or 8 minutes, as the fluid needs to reduce. Strain out your stems, let the mixture cool for a bit, and enjoy!

Plain cannabis tea can taste a bit rough, though, so you might consider adding herbs and sweeteners to your beverage. For tea, mints, lemon, honey, sugar, or any flavoured tea bag can mask the taste. If you're making chai, adding cardamom pods, pepper, and ginger for that traditional zing makes it a tasty and tingly delight.

Marijuana liqueur
Whiskeys, vodkas, or tequilas that are 40% alcohol or more can all dissolve the resin of cannabis. We've got a great recipe for cannabis-infused vodka here, but it's quite a simple process overall.

Decant your chosen alcohol into a mason jar to allow for easier access. Let the stems sit in there for a week or so at a time. By the time you've got another handful of stems ready to add, the old ones will have released their treasures into the mix.

For potency to build, this little project may take a few months and a few handfuls of stems. By the end of the process, though, you'll have a strong cross-fade in one convenient, potent drink.

Thc butter and other edibles

If you have enough broken-down stems to fill up half a saucepan, then THC-infused butter is on the menu! Replacing stems for buds in this cannabutter recipe will produce a similar product, but with a much milder effect. Where the recipe suggests "28g of flowers", replace with "as many chopped stems as possible". Using your butter in culinary creations will add a nice buzz to any course.

Topicals

Perhaps one of the most unconventional ways to enjoy cannabis are weed-infused topicals, which have become quite popular over the past couple of years. Along with moisturising your skin, cannabis-infused lotions and creams can help care for your muscles in a new way. They're also a wonder for supple joints, along with tackling sensitive, red skin especially well. Thankfully, we've already got a recipe for cannabis lotion! Note, however, that you'll be replacing "15–30g of flowers" with 2–3x the amount of stems, or the closest you can get.

Arts and crafts

You might not think about it often, but there's a good bit more you can do with cannabis outside of enjoying its effects. It's a natural plant material like any other, and that means it can see a lot of use in arts and crafts!

Paper

It might sound unconventional at first, but remember that hemp is one of the main alternatives to wood-based paper. Considering that, stem-based paper is far from odd, albeit a bit coarse.

The most challenging part of making paper is first making a vat. This can be pantyhose stretched over a wire armature, or old fly-wire screen stapled to a wooden frame. The idea is to have a flat, permeable surface that will let the water in the pulp drain away.

Then, in a blender, combine an equal amount of stems and regular paper. Add enough water for the mixture to move and blend freely. When the mix is a slurry with minimal bits left intact, pour it out evenly onto the vat. Gently shake the vat until the pulp is evenly spread. If you're making a larger piece of paper, you'll need a squeegee to get things even. Leave this to drain and dry. After 24 hours, gently peel your paper away and hang it out to dry. Trim to your needs, and enjoy!

Weaving small
Even on the small scale, stems and small stalks can be stripped of their outer fibre. This process, called decorticating, involves one of the most sophisticated tools out there: your hands. Held together by a cellulose matrix, these fibres need to be rubbed between the fingers to be separated into individual strands. These

individual lengths of fibres can be twisted into tough lengths of raw twine. If you save up enough, you've got tons of creative possibilities! Might we suggest a tasteful homemade bracelet?

Weaving bigger
The possibilities get even wider, though, if you're a home grower with even more stems lying around. When you strip trunks and main branches of their much longer fibres, you can start making decorations, baskets, and even yarn if you work at it long enough!

Mulch
Capping things off, you can even use your stems to grow yourself some more cannabis! Specifically, you can use a wood chipper (or another processing method) to turn the stems into a reliable mulch. This will protect the soil under it, making sure plants keep as much of their rainwater as possible. There's a lot more information to cover when it comes to properly applying mulch in the growing process, but we hope to have sparked your interest in the idea!

Conclusion

See? There's no need to get mad at the humble stem! There's a world of use to be found if you've got the right supplies, and you can even get high on them if you play your cards right! We hope this has helped you appreciate just how versatile the cannabis plant can be!